The Seaside

by Ru

Falkirk Council

W
FRANKLIN WATTS
LONDON · SYDNEY

Note for parents and teachers

The Changing Times series is soundly based on the requirements of the History Curriculum. Using the device of four generations of a real family, the author combines reminiscences of this family with other people's oral evidence matched with photographs and other contemporary sources. Many other lessons are hidden in the text, which practises the skills of chronological sequencing, gives reference to a timeline and introduces the language and vocabulary of the past. Young children will find much useful information here, as well as a new understanding of the recent history of every day situations and familiar things.

This edition 2004

Franklin Watts
96 Leonard Street
London EC2A 4XD

Franklin Watts Australia
45–51 Huntley Street
Alexandria
NSW 2015

Copyright © 1992 Franklin Watts

Editor: Sarah Ridley
Designer: Michael Leaman
Educational consultant: John West

A CIP catalogue record for this book is available from the British Library.
Dewey Decimal Classification Number: 394.2

ISBN 0 7496 5250 0

Acknowledgements: The author and publishers would like to thank the following people and organisations for their help with the preparation of this book: Anthea Shovelton, Joan Blyth, Sharon Poole of the Woodspring Museum, Weston-super-Mare, John Roles and Hamish MacGillivray of The Royal Pavilion Art Gallery and Museum, Brighton.

Printed in Malaysia

Contents

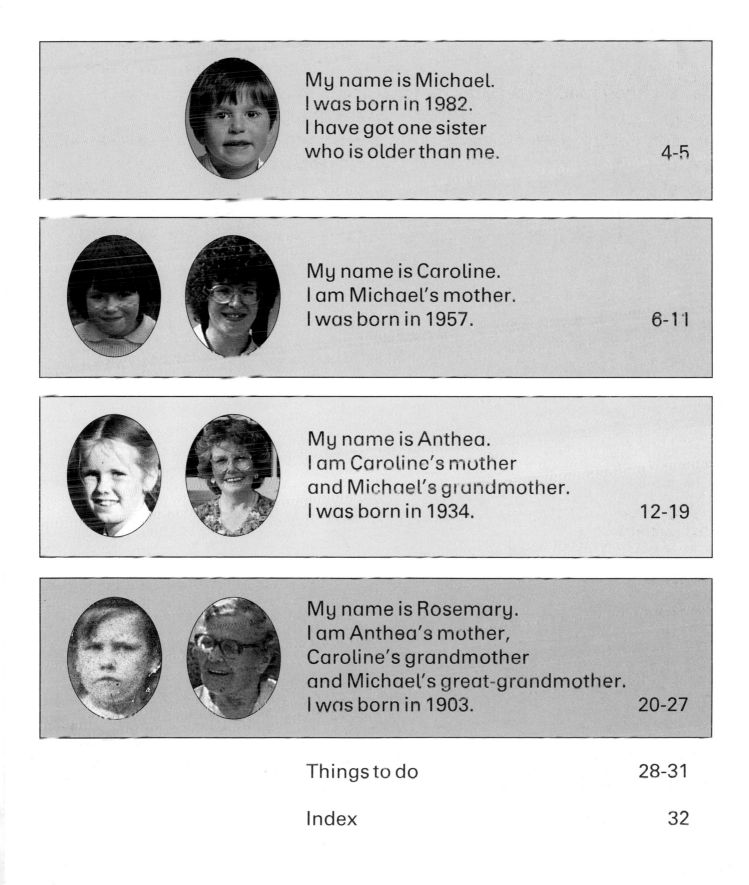

When we go on holiday,
we spend two weeks by the seaside.
Some of my friends go abroad
on package holidays.

We dig in the sand
and paddle in the sea.

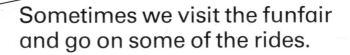

Sometimes we visit the funfair
and go on some of the rides.

We go to the pool
and whizz down
the water slides.

ICE COLD DRINKS

SHAKES
SODAS &
FLOATS

HAMBURGERS   HAMBURGERS   CHEESEBURGERS

HOT FRESH
CHIPS
WITH
BEEFBURGER
ONIONS
AND
BAP

Dad buys popcorn and ice cream
from the stalls on the seafront.

I asked my mum what her holidays were like when she was young.

She told me that they were a bit different from mine.

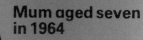

Butlin's FOR YOUR HOLIDAY

She said,

'My first real holiday was at a Butlin's holiday camp. It was fantastic.'

'We stayed in a chalet.'

BUTLIN'S BOGNOR REGIS
Indoor Heated Pool

'The camp had its own funfair and a big swimming pool.'

'There were always things to do.'

'The Redcoats put on games, shows and competitions.'

One year Mum went on holiday to Blackpool.

She said,

'We stayed in a boarding house and went to play on the beach every day.'

8

'Sometimes we walked
along the front.
I'd never seen
so many amusements.'

THE PROMENADE, BLACKPOOL ILLUMINATIONS.

'On the last night
of our holiday,
we were allowed
to stay up late
and see the lights.
They were amazing.'

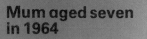
After Mum's sister and brother were born,
her dad bought a caravan.
Then they could go anywhere they pleased.
Every year, they went somewhere different.

Mum said,

'There were always terrible traffic jams as we got near to the coast.'

'Once, we went to Spain for a fortnight. That was the first time I'd ever been on a plane.'

When I asked Grandma about her holidays,
she said her family could never afford a week's holiday.
Her dad wasn't paid if he took time off work.

Eastbourne The

AT WELLS

Local Views Inside

MAKING UP FOR LOST TIME

But they did have bank holiday
day trips with everyone from their street.
Before she was born, her mum and dad
went by charabanc, an open motor coach,
to the seaside.

Later, when Grandma had been born,
they went on trips by motor coach or train.
Once they took the train to Skegness.
There were special cheap fares.

Grandma said,

'On the beach, we all wore
woolly bathing suits.
They were scratchy
and felt heavy
when they got wet.'

'My little brother wore
waterproof paddlers
over his clothes.'

'I had a wooden spade
and a metal bucket.
I played in the sand
for hours.'

'A beach photographer took our picture
and made it into a postcard.'

Grandma said,

'There were always lots of things to do.'

'There were Punch and Judy shows.'

'There were donkey rides.'

'There were children's rides on the pier.'

'The family always bought sticks of rock to take home.'

Grandma said,

'During the war against Germany, the government asked people to stay at home for their holidays.'

'People couldn't go on the beaches. The seafront was fenced off with barbed wire.'

'The soldiers put exploding mines on the beaches, in case the Germans landed.'

'We went to the park
near our house and to the
swimming pool instead.'

When I talked to my great-granny about
her holidays, she said,

'It was a big occasion
for us to go
to the seaside.'

'We went by train
for the day,
dressed in our
Sunday best.'

'No-one ever dreamt of taking off
their clothes on the beach.'

'Girls tucked up their skirts
and boys rolled up their trousers
for paddling.'

1975   1950

Great-granny said,

'We undressed for swimming
inside a bathing machine.
It was wet, sandy and dark.'

'A horse pulled the machine
into the sea. Then we got out
for a dip in the sea.'

'Mostly, we only dipped our feet in the sea.'

'Our biggest treat was going for a ride on a donkey.'

Sea Wall and West Pier, Brighton

"We three are having a jolly time"

'Sometimes we went for a trip along the coast on a paddle steamer. It was always very crowded.'

S. S. Bournemouth Queen.

Great-granny said,   'In the afternoon,
we went for a stroll
along the pier
and the promenade.'

'Grown-ups and children
always had to wear
their hats.'

'We had great fun
putting our money in
the penny-in-the-slot
machines.'

The LATEST GAME of FOOTBALL FOR 2 PLAYERS

INSTRUCTIONS.

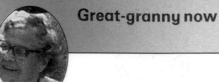
Great-granny said,

'There were all sorts of entertainments.'

'People listened
to music at
the bandstand.'

'Funny pierrots danced and sang.'

'The children watched
Punch and Judy.'

Things to do

Collect some
seaside postcards.

Greetings
from Brighton

IT'S WONDERFUL HERE BY THE SEA !

Southchurch Beach, Southend on Sea.

PAGE'S

Ask your relatives for any old ones they might have.

WE'VE JUST ARRIVED

A BUSY DAY, BLACKPOOL

BOURNEMOUTH BEACH.

Make a seaside scrapbook.

Children now wear beach clothes like these.
Look through the book and find the clothes
your parents and grandparents wore.
What's different about them?

Find out where children in your class go on holiday.
Make a chart like this.

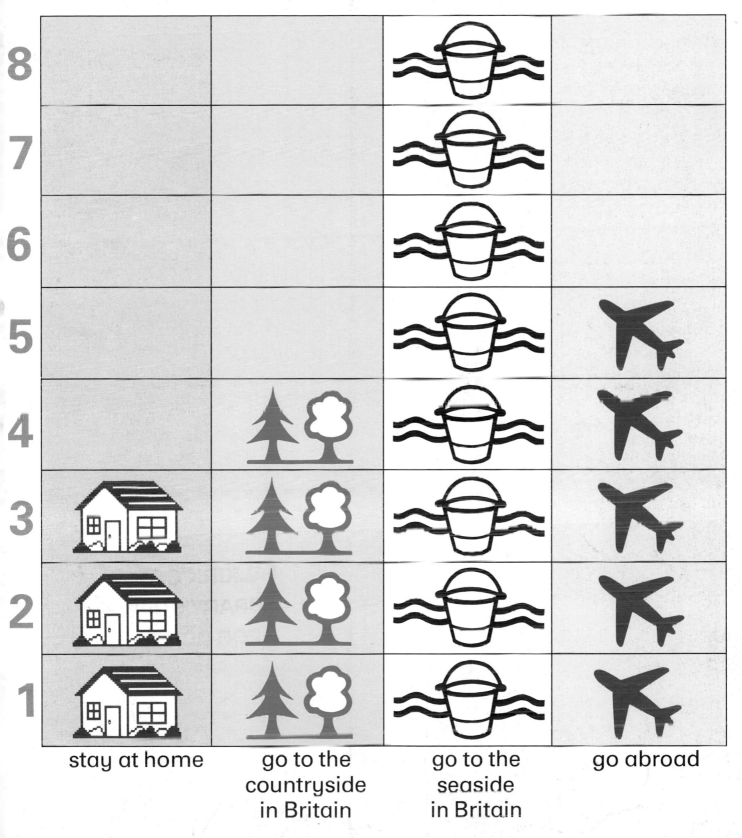

	stay at home	go to the countryside in Britain	go to the seaside in Britain	go abroad
8			🪣	
7			🪣	
6			🪣	
5			🪣	✈
4		🌲🌳	🪣	✈
3	🏠	🌲🌳	🪣	✈
2	🏠	🌲🌳	🪣	✈
1	🏠	🌲🌳	🪣	✈

Index

Photographs: Brighton Reference Library 16(t); The Royal Pavilion Art Gallery and Museum, Brighton cover (tl), 17(t), 22(t), 22(b), 23(t), 27; courtesy of Butlin's Ltd 7(t); Mary Evans Picture Library 19(b); Chris Fairclough Colour Library title page; Francis Frith Collection 12(t), 20-21; Sally and Richard Greenhill 4(1), 4-5(b); Robert Harding Picture Library cover(br), 4-5(ct); Hulton Picture Company 6(b); Imperial War Museum cover(tr), 18 (all); Peter Millard imprint page, 8-9 (background), 14-15 (background), 15(t), 25(bl), 30; National Motor Museum 13(t); National Railway Museum 13(b); Robert Opie 6(tr), 9(t), 11(r); Topham Picture Library cover(bl), 7(b), 8, 10-11, 16(b), 25(t); M J Tozer endpapers; Woodspring Museum Service 10(inset), 15, 24, 25(br); ZEFA 5(r).